this is how the insides of wanting feels
stripped trees and deadened lavender fields
memories of spring
and fresh pillow slips
the anatomy of never being
exactly the perfect fit.

-       the anatomy of wanting

THE
ANATOMY OF
WANTING

Gemma Marie

Cover designed by Sabina Kencana
Instagram @sabinaka

This book is a work of fiction. Names, characters, places, and incidents either are products of the author's imagination or are used fictitiously. Any resemblance to actual persons, living or dead, events, or locales is entirely coincidental.

Gemma Marie
Visit my website at www.poetrybygm.com
Follow me on social media @poetrybygm

Printed in the United Kingdom

First Printing: Aug 2019

ISBN- 9781086344141

to she who keeps on living
even when the pain seemed everlasting-

to she who shelved her fears
even when her soul was reduced to tears-

to she who forever sees the light-
to she who learned to hold on tight-

to she who thought she'd never get there
even after she laid herself bare-

to she who managed to hold on to faith
through what played out as a losing game-

to she who felt forced to chase perfection
the one who despised her own reflection-

to she, to you, to them, to her, to me, to us-

you are enough.

-    dear reader

5

WANTING
PERFECTION

nice house   nice outfit
nice body   nice job
nice family   nice life-

"perfection is mandatory"

we've all had moments of erratic contention
minutes and hours despising our own reflection
years and years of insecurity
putting it down to the stresses of a perfect society-

you are not alone.

–   wanting perfection

the time is 11:04am
i guess that makes me
exactly
eleven hours and four minutes older than at the turn of
today
the first day of autumn
eleven hours and four minutes wiser
than when today turned over.

to the younger me from the turn of the day
don't be afraid today
by the time the sun sets on this fine autumn day
you will have swallowed a thousand different moments
and soothed a million different feelings.

and like the end of every other day
the moon will rise
you will count sheep
and you will go to sleep
knowing you have survived.

- what will you tell yourself this morning?

the hesitation that i write of
is where the river meets the ocean
the doubt of belonging
and the consideration of always-

always being swept along.

-        by something bigger than me

late nights hang beneath my eyes
and that's all i have left
a reflection i thought i knew
now the victim of uncaught theft.

-     who am i?

actually-

maybe we don't want to be found
because we've been lost for so long
this has become home.

-        lost and found

pull out the shovel
and start digging
and keep digging
you're still in there
you
are
still
in
there-

just dig deep.

\-   don't be afraid

dusty soles
and
worn out souls
no mountain was formed for a stroll.

\- have faith that you'll get there

tell yourself secrets
roam free
in the clutter of your mind.

-    learn about you

all those fragments
from the shattering
they might cut your fingers as you collect them from the
floor
but trust me-

this time the puzzle will fit together
much better.

\-   it needed to shatter

weeks go by
not a single cloud in the sky
the turn of every morning
i open my eyes
one at a time
a relief swallows me
the sun still shines
even if only unconsciously
in my forever wanting mind.

-       a blessing

a no is not a wrong decision
it is simply a choice
that says
right now
is not the right time.

\-   maybe later

i am the body of forgiveness
limbs loose but not lifeless
body eased by the art of forgiving
heart beating with the relief of un-needing.

\-   forgive

here i sit
crossed legs on the bed
waiting for tomorrow.

-   a collom lune

an infinite longing for freedom
that moment of escape
is a feeling of exploration
only you can work towards achieving.

- it's within

all it takes is a drop of hope
and the waves of opportunity
will come crashing.

-        oceans of hope

sit and listen to the silences
they hold secrets
you never knew you had.

\-   the key

some of our deepest moments
can exist on the surface
lurking in shallow puddles
just waiting for a tiny bit of light
in preparation of the bloom.

-        sunshine

my thoughts are that of craft
like snowflakes
falling onto a pickaxe
delicate and fragile
yet immaculately mad.

\-   am i making sense?

i whisper to the moon
and she tells me nothing-

nothing more than
'it's time to talk to the sun'.

-        finally

there is no immunity to life
sometimes
rain will come
the grey clouds will crack into a storm
but with wings so strong
i will learn to use them as my shelter.

-      my wings

days when the jar is half empty
is it really just an illusion in my mind?
and the flood gates are opening
filling the jar with fat salty water drops
and then
in the end
the jar is full anyway.

-       perspective

you've come too far to settle
keep sailing that boat
battling through storms
until you hit the shores
of exactly what you're looking for.

-       sailing to freedom

some days only have the purpose
of making us look forward to tomorrow.

-     and that's ok

there's no half measures worthy enough
take that hope
and keep topping it up.

-      half empty or half full?

are we all just paper swans?
forever searching for somewhere to belong-

hiding flaws along seamless folds?
striving for perfection-

with nowhere else to go?

-   paper swans

at your weakest
strive to be stronger
so that one day
even at your weakest
you're stronger than them.

\-   you've got this

she hides her imperfections
inside the perfectly folded lines.

\-   hiding place

those days i tied up fears with rope
over and over again
in the hope
they would drown
amongst the tears
that fell like rain.

\-   tears vs fears

she was her own worst enemy
the corners of her mouth cracking under the pressure
eyelids dancing as they flickered holding tight
her soul dissolving more each day-

everything seems different through an unplugged
mind.

-    unplugged or over plugged?

be the change you need to see
dig deep
dream big
discover who you want to be.

-       not just a dreamer

embrace the fails
trust me when i say
you're the only one over watching.

-      nobody else noticed

nerves are only a sign
sent to tell you-

you're out of your comfort zone
you're pushing your boundaries
your heart is pounding
you are alive.

-        embrace it

she was a goddess-

the queen of her own tiny waterfalls
that gathered in puddles
along uncensored bones.

\-   tears

the silent pounding
of blood jumping
the line between sanity and rotting-

pouring back spells
of sapphire warmth-

the chasing and biting
and aching and longing-

the sudden rush
of unforgotten wanting.

-       deafening

once upon a time i was waiting
waiting for opportunities
waiting for life
waiting for happiness-

how foolish the unknowing heart can be.

\-   just waiting

amongst reflections
that dance on shallow waters
unfaulted by currents
undisturbed by raindrops
my soul preys on abandoned strength
left in solace by the tamed shrew.

\-   searching

when she is not her
breaths shallow weep in abandonment
and her heart feels a weakness
that crumbles like empty bullet holes
to a derelict building.

\-   empty

along the purgatory of paper folds
lays the seamless desperation
for perfection.

\-   lines

if we woke up today
depleted of personalities
aneamic to dreams
wouldn't the world be a sad place?

-       bleeding dreams

perfection is crooked
tangled and broken
an escape to the necessity
of the often unspoken.

\-   what is perfection?

why does she strive so hard
to achieve something her heart doesn't need?

why did it take so long to realise
the inner her was desperate to be freed?

\-   timeless

inside the madness
lays a relentless need
for space to grieve
corseted shut
by her own apologies.

\-   don't be so hard on yourself

a heart framed by mist
once inhaled as a friend
can now no longer exist-

i huff and i puff
tongue loose in my mouth
and there you stay
i can't seem to let you out.

-        lost words

it has saved me
the irony of its exquisite flaws
the beautiful faults along its lined seams
hiding immaculately along unseen folds
and realising
that is reality.

-       everything is not as it seems

and if the search for perfection were a pain
it would be the slice
of the most carefully folded seam
the gasp and the droplet
that would follow for a while
and ultimately the vanishing
as if it never even existed.

-      temporary

what tires me-

tossing the ball in the court of my imagination
sentimental games
with no certainties
other than the sky crashing down
and raining off my sanity.

-       that's what tires me

glittering traces of optimism
gather along the lines of ancient frowns
a heart-warming wisdom sparkles through the
parts of her
she once hated.

-        through the feet of crows

it's hard to imagine
how dull a world would be
where perfection
actually existed.

\-   don't you think?

this time the paper folds perfectly
symmetrical lines
smoothed by soft fingers
a graceful swan
just as she felt.

-       perspective of perfection

once i was a girl
mouth full of silences
throat cut
by the blade
of grass dripping a dew of my secrets
until the anonymous morning
littered my hopes like seeds
and through the flutters of wind
came the first whistle.

-      new beginnings

goddess-
of silenced wonder
a tongue born to be bitten
and never to surrender-

the day dawn broke
through haze and through sorrow
she danced down silk canals
made an escape to tomorrow-

goddess(es)-
of unhinged whispers
souls to be heard
come and dance with us.

-       goddess

expectations
(like) the wind that carried me for so long.

-      not anymore

does a caged bird
beg you to open the summer window?

or does he wait
for his own perfect moment
to trespass into freedom?

\-   real perfection

when you start to see beauty in unlikely places
then you'll know
you're already healing.

-       it's a process

what are you dying for?
dying to be?
chasing the skeletons of desire
ogling graves plucked of daisies
be careful not to slip
after all
the inside is dug deep
and the clock ticks on-
tick tock, tick tock.

\-   what is it you're striving for?

maybe this is where gratitude resides?
wrapped up in the wool of a well-worn jumper
believing she can fight the bite
of a lost summer.

\-   lady gratitude

we need to stop saying
we want to be perfect-

for what is perfect?

childlike dreams
that stick to the lips like candy floss-

age when the wisdom in lines
lay as deep as the litter filled ocean-

youth with a bursting naivety
that dances carelessly around empty playgrounds-

beauty that comes to haunt you in the night-

we need to stop seeking perfection-

for what is it?
if not only the very moment we are living in.

-      does it even exist?

you are not perfect
nor am i
today is the day
perfection
becomes the world's most immaculate lie.

-      fake

WANTING
HAPPINESS

she's happy *he's happy*
they're happy *so happy*

"happiness is a requirement"

we've all had days of feeling lost
lots of nights
not feeling enough
lots of winters
spent in fear
summers lost to endless tears-

you are not alone.

\-   wanting happiness

the time is 8:08am
that makes it exactly eight hours and eight minutes into
this new morning
the very first morning
of a very first day
of a very new year-

to the younger me of yesteryear-

enjoy this year
embrace its gifts
don't be afraid of its flaws
learn about yourself
forgive others-

for today isn't the first day of january-

it is the first hours of any day
the first days of any month-

today is the day
you wake up
and make the decision-

this is the beginning of your own new year.

-       what will you tell yourself this morning?

today remember
the journey is the most fun
the destination is beautiful and longed for
but take a look-

the journey is preparing you
growing you
for your arrival.

\-   are you ready?

is purpose a feeling of fulfilment?

like how she
the mountain feels after she is climbed-

does she share the moment
with she who climbed her?

high up, on a high
above the world-

where the only thing to feel
is the that of flying-

and that feeling
is completely natural.

-      flying high

drink tea with the skeletons
that make your closet
their home.

\-   inner peace

an arrangement of letters
that only echo
the reared head of a slayed dragon-

for she who flies
may again translate the letters to
fight again.

-       typos

when i think of flowers
i think of ghosts
floating above manicured graves-

of time gone by
where an old me lays-

i think of honeybees
and sticky summer evenings-

a brand new me
and reborn beginnings.

-      reinvention

fear is a friend
disguised as the devil
but give him time
and you will see
that fear only teaches us
how to take his hand
and let him guide us into a world
where we can be free.

-       sometimes we have to take a risk

forgiveness is like dawn
it grows and becomes brighter
until finally
what you're forgiving
is nothing but dusk.

\-   it gets easier

resist the fall onto the thorns
that some days present
breathe
smell the flowers
touch the petals instead.

\-   a flower story

that's not your brain malfunctioning
that's your mind adapting
switching gears
pulling you through.

\- trust it

weeks go by
not a single cloud in the sky
the turn of every morning
i open my eyes
one at a time
a relief swallows me
the sun still shines
even if only unconsciously
in my forever wanting mind.

-       dawn break

you are the composer
of your own melodies.

\-   music of the heart

weep salt crushed pearls
so beautiful
you're proud to wear them around your neck.

-    tears are strength

she is soft
blankets of fallen gold leaves-

she is tough
punnets of conkers
plucked from the trees-

she is strong
swirls of squirrels that tease-

autumn envelopes her
like toffee
sickly and sweet-

the summer is over and this year
she won't even grieve.

-   seasons change

beauty is for everyone
it lives in your heart
ready to project wherever you want it
but first
you have to believe it's there.

\-   you are beautiful

if she were a colour
could she be only one?

yesterday she was navy
as dark as the night-

today she is yellow
a sunflower
open and bright-

tomorrow who knows
what colour she will feel-

but who needs to stay one way anyway-

as long as she feels real.

- be you

under the sparkling sky
when no one is around
i lay down
and play out
all the happiness i have found.

-        alone time

without a single noise
you cross me
a shadow of jet
a prowl of confidence
and if i were superstitious
i'd think today was going to be a good one.

-       (not a bad one)

be the sun-
some days she is weaker
but she always bounces back.

be the sun-
some days are lighter
some are darker.

be the sun-
because no matter what
she always turns up
strong and bright
and high on life.

\-   lessons from the sun

every day i chase the sun
just to try and catch its rays in my hands
to collect its beams
and fill my empty jar
with glimmers of hope.

-        positivity

some days i feel like the moon
trying hard to light up
amongst her darkness-
i am cold to the touch
lifeless.

but the moon doesn't feel like me
she's strong and playful
an imperfect crescent
an inconsistent glimmer-
she's happy that way.

she shows up every night
without fail
every single time the darkness falls.

-       lessons from the moon

as the clock strikes his bells of midnight
amongst the thick blanket of night
breathe
sleep
be kind
only a few more chimes
until comes the morning light.

-    it's coming

bruised knees (bruised ego)
wild hair (wild mind)
bleeding elbows (bleeding heart)
wrinkled eyes (wrinkled thoughts)

our bodies are just the shells that take us on our journey.

-       soul vs body

run through the flares
orange crackles
run through the fire
fear rattles
run through the rain
to dampen the burn
and then sit and reflect
there was something to learn.

- lessons in happiness

back then i was a riot of flamingos
the kind of riot that is fierce in feed
but calm in wade-

a journey with the strength
of a one-legged race.

-       not anymore

i act this way when i run out of smiles
when the dawn takes too long to arrive and the dusk
lingers around my mind
dancing in suffocation
when i need to take a step outside
so i can peer through the window
like i am just me
yet i am nothing
but
the rest of us.

- just me

in this moment
everything is right
in this moment
you're living in the light
in the next moment
hold on to that feeling
in every moment
believe in what you're being.

-       believe in yourself

what is the face of gravity
if not that of a duck
swimming fluidly to nowhere but a place at the end of the
river
the estuary of life
where she will never topple over
but wade effortlessly
feet forever underwater.

- gravity

don't be afraid to peel back the sun's rays
like brushed cotton sheets
climb in
finally
cocoon yourself in the warmth and comfort you deserve.

\-   security

it's real
those feelings
they were real
over time they become memories
that feel less real
but know they happened
and learn to treasure the memories
that make you just so.

\-   memories

sunshine through blankets of clouds
peeking through
and shining down
i missed those days
through loss and pain
but this morning i awoke
and you shine down on me again.

-       new day

surrounding yourself with positivity
is not only a game changer
it's a mind changer.

-        goodbye negativity

rolling around
like a marble in my fist
slippery and sliding
and warm to my caress-

it hasn't always been here
i never held it tight
but now i won't let go
of this handful of light.

       -    caught it

have you finally forgotten
the trouble it is
to be plagued
by the feeling of awake?

-      insomnia

and if i ever become removed again
now i know
the bittersweet taste of the elixir of life
will once again be my medicine.

-        irony

i could see it moving that day
approaching the shore
as the clouds moved away-

unveiling the twinkles
calming the tides
and finally surrounding me
in long awaited light.

\-   realisation

some days we are nothing but a space of pain
drowning ourselves in the unforgiving rain-

those days will pass and wash away
leaving behind the blooming fragrance of today.

\-   a fresh morning

hedonism is sunday's child
unfussy in its preparation
of what may or may not come.

-        the unknown

at the end of it all
we do nothing
but
push up stems of headless daisies.

-     life

with my life
i promise cries of explicit
with my heart
i promise to illicit-

nothing but power
in tears and in love
even when the times
inevitably become tough.

\-   a promise

it pains me when you can't smile
when your mind is smashed up
even for a while-

remember
hold your head high
feel the self-worth
look up to the sky
and put yourself first.

-       please

this morning
take a moment
to look-

stand on the side-line
of your life
and admire how far you've come-

no matter how long it took.

-   admire yourself

sometimes i wish
i could see more clearly
i wish
the light would come and save me
sometimes i wish
to be rescued
i wish
the sun would set
on the infinite chase of gratitude.

-       but it'll be worth it

the rougher the terrain
the trustier the boots that got you there.

-        you are tough

embrace the twisted lines
and wobbly curves
the over thought 'yes'
and the under thought 'no'
embrace the drowning desire for mercy
the wrenching hope
and the gutter of doubt
that are merely the outlines
of everything that is you.

\-   human

hope wants me to unzip the past.

-        of course she does

it's hard to say exactly where wonder hangs her hat
she bangs on doors
waiting patiently for you to open
she lays gasping for breath in the bottomless ocean
but she never gives up
as seasons change
she waits for you
patiently with love
and as if the solstice will never come.

\-   where is wonder?

maybe you just don't see
the rainbow effect of mosaics
the colours that the sky bled
into puddles on the ground
and when the sun came out
it turned into rainbow glass
sharp, beautiful and yours to be found.

-       change

saint bird of choir
if i fall to my knees
in prayer
will you fly me away with you?

-      flight

the damsel in distress-

forever raising her head
but these days we are friends-

today she's an honorary guest.

- once a damsel

it is not shameful
to create a world
that makes you happy-

you are the gateway to your own wonderland.

\-   enjoy it

some days i am more storm
than full lungs
and beating heart
hair wild as an unfound boar
eyes bright like fireflies
through the black stretch of night
i soak to the bone
bounded by fear of repetition.

-       unbound me

this is the season i learn to breathe deep
this is the evening i learn not to weep
this is the morning i open my eyes
this is the moment my heart beats with pride
this is the year i thought i'd never see
this is the time to set myself free.

-       now is the time

WANTING
LOVE

love is wonderful   *love is heartbreak*
she's in love   *he's in love*
they're in love   *love is blind*

"love yourself first"

we've all held other hearts in our hands
had ours smashed
lost faith in romance
every one of us fell out of love with ourselves
then fell back in
because that's how love goes-

you are not alone.

-        wanting love

the time is 11:11am
i forever see double numbers
does that make me a believer
or for infinity
 a dreamer?

if you are reading this
know that in this exact moment
you have survived a million moments
and all those moments you have survived
have already passed
and by the time you finish reading this
another moment will have passed
even the moments that hurt
will pass
always know that.

-        what will you tell yourself this morning?

is love meant to feel
like a rolling boil of emotion
counting only
the seconds that come
before the overspill
that sizzles the fire?

\-   i've forgotten

maybe your heart is smashed into a thousand pieces
a million pieces
a billion pieces
you're the only one counting.

\-   strength

the creator of repulsion
is attraction
and the radicalness of its inorganic manifestation
and if we hold arrows
it is born from missing the bullseye
the spherical space
of what is deemed
singular perfection.

-     arrows

if i hadn't opened my mouth
would you have swallowed me whole?

-     no more silence

sweet words stain the mind
be kind.

-       please

a stranger
is a holder of nothingness
a silent observer
with sewn lips
and fleets of unknown opinions
that park in a mind
you do not know.

\-   love you

passenger seat empty of borrowed time
i tilt my head and through the grime-

i wipe away the dust of sleeping earth
inhale the scent of frosty turf-

i gaze-

and in this valley of wonder
carry me
and pull me under-

before the thunder
crashes-

and wakes us up.

-      dreamer

some people will try to use their powers
to extract your magic
ignore them
keep casting your spells.

-     we are all magic

roots that float stable through air
skin that is tough from evaporated rain
weathered by storms
wounds healed by berry red pickings
and a blackbird's morning song.

a reminder
you are a forest
defying gravity
surviving destruction.

\-   nature's way

my heart is more passion than love
my lungs are more hope than air
my mind is more chaos than sanity
and
that's what makes me human.

-       your go

no one else will light the candle
to guide you through the darkness.

-       only you

at nightfall you will find me
collecting the wax that drips
silently
from your flickering light
and like a dawn that will never arrive
i will rebuild the candle
i need to guide me
all through the night.

-       work for it

maybe foolish am i
to believe
that in the heady space of love
you'd be my congestion
of joy
for always.

\-   a foolish heart

where the swallowed webs of lies do linger
i wrap the lace around my finger
lonely notes of a drenched-up past
i can only hope
this feeling won't last.

-        old feelings

quite honestly
it tastes like stardust-

mystical and like it never existed.

-       did it exist?

from what once was a beginning
spun a web of existence
frost that was too heavy to hold
the fascination in the broken
the definition of endings
a feeling that will never grow old.

-       endings

as she sighs
between the lies
dormant poison
remain the only ties.

-        poison(ed)

like a picnic of memories
feasted on a patchwork quilt
sewn through snippets
of a time gone by-

now i will always gorge on peace
because-

i forgive you.

-       forgiveness

if i save you
will you save me too?

-        will you?

it is not possible to be completely broken
with wings so resilient.

- fly

even the most vibrant rose
can't help but wilt
without sun and water.

-        self care

every single memory
is nourishment
your heart deserves.

\-   don't be afraid of them

we were young then
invincible
frozen in eternity
fools to forever.

-       things change

you deserve to be understood
you deserve to be that aching, empty space to someone
when you're gone.

-       value

if forever never comes-
then i'll take today.

-     holding a moment

maybe truth is the key
to the door that's been so hard to open.

-        maybe?

melt me like candle wax
inflicted by your fire
let me shape and mould
into what i truly desire.

-       please let me

a brave dive to see what lies beneath
bitter water
steals her breath
she dives deep into the realms of clarity
soft fins
a sudden mellow
the gentle stroke of a newfound tail
and finally-

a new direction.

\-   mermaid

lavender haze
fresh
warm
and there i laze
free
untorn-

it was only a matter of time all along.

- good things come to those who wait

we are mountains of old
lush, soft outsides
insides of stone, cold
saluting the sun, sizzling bright
blinded
and searching for the light.

-      know this

no apologies anymore
for fresh silence-

spells of freedom
laced in the scents of clarity-

just me
and this transparent happiness.

- finally

looking back is ok
treasure your lessons
ache
feel
taste
but never, ever regret.

-        never

some days i view life through honey glazed eyes
blurred and unwanting
yet fatefully rimmed
with a tender, sweet offering.

\-   sweet

and if i were only a pit of blackened silence
would you forgive my inexplicable sorrow
and intertwine my empty mind
with the lost daisies of spring?

-      just a thought

inside my heart
is a constellation of hopes
pumping through my blood
with the rush of a forbidden galaxy.

\-   never stop hoping

secrets stitched along seemingly perfect seams
temptation like tired endings
pleading for forgiveness
begging for rebirths
needing to be rewritten.

-        forgiving

not to be fooled by conviction
she grew from being small
to push in a direction
one last blink would confirm the resilience
a tear dropped hard
a testimony to her brilliance.

-       crystal cut tear drops

the dusk is a deliverer
of heart shaped lanterns.

-        if you let it be

maybe we're living in a world of assumed purity
frantically hiding
soles and palms that are dirty-

hoping we don't get caught out by our cries
and don't get plagued by burning eyes.

-       what are you looking at?

don't let them convince you
that your lines must be straight
and your curves must be rounded
don't let them convince you
that you have to be better than you.

-       some will try

and if you run
then i can no longer pray
that you'll come back-

wrists torn
feet worn
because finally
my mind tells me
you're already gone.

\-   doubt

among the flames
that burn at the dawn of tomorrow-

the desire
that fogs the nightingale's eye-

the crushing grief of time gone by-

you have everything to give.

-       believe it

like a time that is fleeting
a petal that is floating
your presence is only in another dimension to now
(here)
one dictated by a sundial
and celestial bodies
you are nothing but a shadow to me.

-      that is all

goodbye no longer means
the end
it's just the beginning of a new chapter.

-       don't worry

home is a passing summer evening
an envelope of warmth from a fire setting sun
a pool of forgotten sorrows
a night of magic laced dreams.

\-   home is whatever you want it to be

your fingerprints
are scars
i can only hope
never fade.

- wanting

with a single breath
caught between the untold death
of a once yellow dandelion-

i'm caught in the wind
that carries me towards you.

-       fate

she says that paradise is him
that as the haze of the morning lifts from silent canals
the prayers of the day
the divinity of him
stain her every being with the promises of home.

-    home

i live for sunday mornings
and air littered with the smell of fallen leaves
for sunrises i no longer eagerly await
and sunsets i'm no longer afraid of
i live for heady summer times and crisp winter times
and carousels that carry my dreams
around and around and around.

-        how things change

and when your heart pounds so hard
it leaps from your chest
chase it.

-        it wants you to

i will tie my arteries in bows
to stop the feeling of peace ever leaving
until i see you again
ready to un-parcel my heart back to you.

-    it's yours

conqueror of her demons
capturer of his heart.

\-   princess

and if the moon
is truly a ruler of our emotions
then i will blame its eclipse
and banished light
when i run to you
through fallen towers.

-     blindly

as this evening falls-

my eyes are the keepers of sunsets
and yours-

are the keepers of my heart.

-        dusk

the map like a line drawing
of our constellations
a pencil tip circling
the outline of existence
a contagion of
you, me, this, us.

\-   feelings

i like you
like the planets
aligned yet scattered-

like earth
rotating blindly on her axis-

i like you
like constellations of stars that surround us-

like meteors that hurdle
and shower us in lust-

like debris
that we will never know what it consists of-

in a universe we will never understand-

lonesome in a galaxy
where you take my hand.

\-   i like you

with a monochrome love
i am buried deep beneath untold skin
there is no grey area in this future
just a simple black or white
here or (and) now.

\-   monochrome

everything i do
is not for the end-

like the table
empty on one side-

and the space between us
that feels like infinity-

it is not for the end-

it is to hold on to the beginning of you
and the forever bursting middle of us-

because in this weightless space
there is never an end-

only end(less) moments of joy.

-          end(less)

pour me a life
of silk streamed happiness.

\-   i'm waiting

i come from a dream
a vision of presence-

one where i lay
with serpents and pheasants-

i come from a life
of millions of paces-

a journey sometimes weak
with condemned empty spaces-

i come from a yesterday
where the pendulum struck-

i defeated the avalanche
and then there you stood-

i come from a morrow
where you and i march-

through gardens of obscure
with love in our hearts-

we come from a phenomenon
a conjured-up world-

one that is ours
no one else can unfold.

-        a fairy tale

dear you,

we are gifted tomorrow
to peel ourselves open
to drench ourselves in the pulp of today-

to dissect the anatomy of lies that is perfection
to understand the soft insides of happiness
to learn that internal love is the key to external love-

and the lessons in which we learn to no longer want-

but simply to live-

to be you, imperfectly
to be happy, endlessly
to be loved, unconditionally.

with love,
me.

ALSO BY

Gemma Marie

SCREAMING WINGS

'your wings can't fly you
into the depths of your future
if your feet are still tied down
by the strings of your past.'

Inspired by one girl's journey to freedom from the rat race lifestyle, this debut collection of poetry and prose from author *Gemma Marie* promises a soul soothing read.

Every single one of the 180 contemporary poems have been carefully written to help the reader overcome self-doubt, negativity and to provide hope, light and positivity to anyone who needs it.

Through her words, the author hopes to inspire others to break free from society's norms and join her on a journey to freedom.

Available worldwide on Amazon.